IN THE BEGINNING GOD

CREATED THE HEAVENS

AND THE EARTH.

- GENESIS 1:1

THE SPIRIT REALM OF GOD

BY CORY VOSSPETER

THE SPIRIT REALM OF GOD

Copyright © 2024 by Cory Vosspeter

Unless otherwise identified, Scripture quotations are from the New King James Bible (NKJ).

ISBN: 978-0-473-72717-8

Contact:: Cory Vosspeter per Email at CVosspeter@gmail.com

Introduction

This book is written to bring <u>photographic evidence</u> of the existence of God, Jesus Christ, angels, the demonic forces and the spiritual realms. In this book I share my personal experiences that I had with the Lord God, the Angels, as well as the demonic spirits.

I hope that this book opens the spiritual eyes of the believers and unbelievers alike, and draws them closer to Jesus Christ. The truth is, heaven and hell are real places which we enter as spirit beings after we die, having all our senses.

Please seek the truth, read the Word of God, and ask the Lord Jesus Christ to reveal himself to you. Turn from your wicked ways, repent, and be saved from eternal suffering.

Also while living in New Zealand, I received many dreams and visions about the coming of God's judgements. The prophetic dreams and visions that I have received, I share in the last chapter of this book.

Thank You

Thank you, Lord Jesus, for laying your life down for all of us, dying on the cross so we can have forgiveness for our sins, and eternal life with you.

I also thank you Lord for the gifts you have given me. Let them be used for your glory and for the advancement of the Kingdom of Heaven. Let your truth be known and your glory fill the earth. Holy Spirit please breeze upon the pages of this book, so that many will see, believe and be saved.

I like to thank my beautiful son Jacob-Isaiah for his love , help and support.

Table of Contents

MY STORY

I was born in 1963 in Germany; at the age of three, I started seeing into the spirit realm. As I grew older, it became more frequently. I began seeking information about the supernatural. I read books about ghosts, angels and the paranormal, seeking answers. I watched TV shows about ghost hauntings and the New Age beliefs. This led to demonic encounters, as things started to move around in our Apartment. After seeking God in 1987, God, in his mercy, sent an Angel in physical form to me, to save my life and my soul from eternal damnation. Shortly after the angelic encounter, my husband and I left Germany in 1989 and moved to Canada. We immigrated to Canada in 1989, where he accepted Christ. We were water-baptized and spirit-filled, serving God in the local Church. In 1995, I attended Bible College, and we served in the local Church and outreaches in Windsor, Ontario, Canada, and Detroit, Michigan, USA. From 1997 to 2005 I attended a prophetic training school in Trenton, Michigan. The physical angelic encounters continued in Canada and now also in New Zealand. In 2005, my son and I moved to New Zealand. When we arrived in New Zealand, I started having dreams and visions of places where, in the past, blood had been spilled. The Word of God says, "The blood is crying out from the ground (Gen.4:10)."

<u>Prayer from 2 Corinthians 4:1 - 4 NKJV</u>

Therefore seeing we have this ministry, as we have received mercy, we faint not; but have renounced the hidden things of dishonesty, not walking in craftiness, nor handling the Word of God deceitfully; but by manifestation of the truth commending ourselves to every man's conscience in the sight of God. But if our gospel be hid, it is hid to them that are lost, in whom the god of this world hath blinded the minds of them which believe not, lest the light of the glorious gospel of Christ, who is the image of God, should shine unto them.

And so I pray that the Lord God would open your spiritual eyes and understanding. To give you sight to see the unseen spirit realm, that is presented here in this book. That the unbeliever might be saved, in the name of Jesus Christ I pray.

The Story, God's Son "Jesus Christ"

By Cory Vosspeter

God the Father is Spirit

This book is written for all who doubt the existence, of God the Father, Jesus Christ, angels, and the heavenly realm, as well as, the demonic realm. In 2005, I was given the gift of spiritual photography so that anyone who doubts that the Word of God is the truth, might see and believe. He is the Creator of the Universe, and everything that is within it. The earth, it's dimensions, and its occupants, are made by Him for him. God is a spirit being, and so are all of God's Angels. All the fallen angels, demons, evil spirits, are spirit beings and are not seen by human eyes. When we believe in Jesus Christ's existence and sacrifice through the shedding of His blood, we will receive forgiveness for our sins and be given a new spiritual life. And since we are created in God's image, we are tri beings, flesh, soul and spirit. (Genesis 1:1-31). Angels are ministering spirits; they are not limited to the spirit realm. Angels can assume human form and perform human deeds. Angels are immortal beings and invisible to human eyes. Once we accept Jesus Christ as our Saviour, we are redeemed believers and the veil of our sin is removed. When God sees it fit, we can feel and sometimes see the angelic. We can have a relationship with the Father through Jesus Christ and with the help of the Holy Spirit. Through the daily reading of the Word of God and prayer, we will hear His voice leading us. Sometimes, we can entertain Angels unaware and could be experiencing an angelic visitation. In my book, I share my experiences that I had with the Lord and his Angels, as well with the demonic spirits.

God the Father is Spirit

-2-

Colossians 1:16-17 NKJV: "For by Him, all things were created in heaven and on earth, visible and invisible, whether thrones or dominions or principalities or powers. All things were made through Him for him. And He is before all things, and in Him all things consist".

God the Father has revealed himself in different ways through His Son Jesus Christ, His Spirit, dreams, visions, personal experiences, and angelic encounters.

Jesus Christ became the perfect blood sacrifice, the Passover lamb, who died for mankind's sins on the cross. Jesus died on Passover before the Sabbath would start, Friday sundown.

Scripture references: (John 11: 55 - 57, 13: 1- 38; 19: 31- 36)

Scripture Reference NKJV God is Spirit. **(John 4:21 – 24 NKJV)**
Jesus said to her, "Woman, believe Me, the hour is coming when you will neither on this mountain, nor in Jerusalem, worship the Father. "You Samaritans worship what you do not know; we worship what we do know, for salvation is from the Jews." "But the hour is coming, and now is, when the true worshipers will worship the Father in spirit and in truth; for the Father is seeking such to worship Him."

The Story, God 's Son "Jesus Christ "

Our story starts in Genesis when God created humans, He made male and female.

Genesis 1: 27- 30 NKJV So God created man in His own image; in the image of God He created him; <u>male and female</u> He created them. God <u>blessed them</u> and said to them, "<u>Be fruitful and increase in number</u>; fill the earth and subdue it. Rule over the fish in the sea and the birds in the sky and over every living creature that moves on the ground." And God said, "See, I have given you every herb that yields seed which is on the face of all the earth, and every tree whose fruit yields seed; to you it shall be for food. Also, to every beast of the earth, to every bird of the air, and to everything that creeps on the earth, in which there is life, I have given every green herb for food"; and it was so.

NOTE: This was not Adam and Eve. It is my belief that God created the indigenous people first.

The Garden of God ; " Eden " was created for one man called Adam, for God's fellowship with a human.

The Story, God 's Son "Jesus Christ "

Here is the evidence that God had created other humans before creating Adam and Eve.

Genesis 4: 14 - 17 NKJV we read here that God send Cain out of His presence because he killed his brother Able.

(14) I shall be a fugitive and a vagabond on the earth, and it will happen that anyone who finds me will kill me."

(15) And the Lord said to him, "Therefore, whoever kills Cain, vengeance shall be taken on him sevenfold." And the Lord set a mark on Cain, lest anyone finding him should kill him.

(16) And Cain knew his wife, and she conceived and bore Enoch. And he build a city, and called the name of the city after the name of his son — Enoch.

(17) And so we read about Cains family from here on and the first created people.

The Story, God's Son "Jesus Christ"

Genesis 2:7- 9 NKJV "ADAM" And the Lord God formed man of the dust of the ground, and **breathed into his nostrils the breath of life; and man became a living being,** (filled with God's Spirit, His breath). The Lord God planted a garden eastward in Eden, and there He put the man whom He had formed. And out of the ground the Lord God made every tree grow that is pleasant to the sight and good for food. The tree of life was also in the midst of the garden, <u>and the tree of the knowledge of good and evil.</u>

Genesis 2:15 - 17 NKJV Then the Lord God took the man and put him in the garden of Eden to tend and keep it. And the Lord God commanded the man, saying, "Of every tree of the garden you may freely eat; but of the tree of the knowledge of good and evil you shall not eat, for in the day that you eat of it you shall surely die ."
(And spiritually they died after eating the fruit of the tree of good and evil).

Genesis 2:21 – 22 NKJV EVE was created. And the Lord God said, "It is not good that man should be alone; I will make him a helper comparable to him." And the Lord God caused a deep sleep to fall on Adam, and he slept; and He took one of his ribs, and closed up the flesh in its place. 22 Then the rib which the Lord God had taken from man He made into a woman, and He brought her to the man.

(This is the creation of Adam and Eve in the garden east of Eden, for the fellowship with an eternal God and Father).

The Story, God's Son "Jesus Christ "

Now after Satan in a form of a snake deceived Eve and then also Adam. A just God had to fell judgement on them and on Satan, the snake. Adam and Eve who were clothed in the glory of God, they lost the covering. God the Father had to kill two sheep to fashion a covering for the now two naked people. This was the first blood sacrifice and covenant that our heavenly Father made with his creation, man. (Genesis 3 : 1– 29 NKJV)

The Lord God made for Adam and his wife tunics of skin, and clothed them. Then the Lord God said, "Behold, the man has become like one of us, to know good and evil. And now, lest he put out his hand and take also of the tree of life, and eat, and live forever". Therefore the Lord God sent him out of the garden of Eden, to till the ground from which he was taken. So He drove out the man; <u>and He placed a Cherubim at the east of the garden of Eden, and a flaming sword which turned every way, to guard the way to the tree of life.</u>
(Eden is in the spirit realm that lies beyond our earthly realm).

This was the first blood sacrifice and blood covenant between God and his creation.

And with this, humans lost the eternal life and the ability to fellowship with an eternal Father. Eternal life and fellowship with our heavenly Father would be restored through, the sacrifice and death of Jesus Christ, God's Son. He would become the ultimate blood sacrifice, a lamb so pure, without sin. And a man, without sin that would die in our place and restore all that was lost in the garden of Eden.

The Story, God's Son "Jesus Christ "

Before we can visit with Jesus Christ we must look at the **second important blood sacrifice and covenant in Exodus**. We start at the place and time when the Jewish people had to prepare the Passover celebration, and were delivered out of bondage.

Exodus 12 : 1 - 28 NKJV Then Moses called for all the elders of Israel and said to them, "Pick out and take lambs for yourselves according to your families, and kill the Passover lamb. And you shall take a bunch of hyssop, dip it in the blood that is in the basin, and strike **the lintel and the two doorposts with the blood** that is in the basin. And none of you shall go out of the door of his house until morning. For the Lord will pass through to strike the Egyptians; and when **He sees the blood on the lintel and on the two doorposts,** the Lord will pass over the door and not allow the destroyer to come into your houses to strike you. And you shall observe this thing as an ordinance for you and your sons forever.

This was the second important blood sacrifice and blood covenant between God and man.

Jesus Christ is the door to which we enter into salvation and eternal life.

John 10:9 - I am the door, if anyone enters by Me, he will be saved, and will go in and out find pasture. (NKJV). This is eternal salvation through Jesus Christ's sacrifice on the cross.

The Story, God's Son "Jesus Christ "

With the blood on the lintel and doorposts, it was a sign that Jesus would shed His blood for us and that He will become the door to the Father, salvation and eternal life.

We now visit with Jesus Christ and look at the third blood covenant and blood sacrifice.

The story starts in Matthew 1:18 - 23 NKJV. Now the birth of Jesus Christ was as follows: After His mother Mary was betrothed to Joseph, before they came together, she was found with child of the Holy Spirit. But while he thought about these things, behold, an Angel of the Lord appeared to him in a dream, saying, "Joseph, son of David, do not be afraid to take to you Mary as your wife, for that which is conceived in her is of the Holy Spirit. And she will bring forth a son, and you shall call his name Jesus, for he will save his people from their sins." So all this was done that it might be fulfilled which was spoken by the Lord through the prophet, saying: "Behold, the virgin shall be with child, and bear a son, and they shall call His name **Emmanuel," which is translated, "God with us."** Then Joseph, being aroused from sleep, did as the Angel of the Lord commanded him and took Mary as his wife. Joseph did not know his wife until she had brought forth her firstborn son, and he called His name Jesus.

As Mary was a virgin until the birth of Jesus, for no man had entered her. This was the new blood covenant between God and his creation.

The Story, God's Son "Jesus Christ"

Jesus Christ, became the blood sacrifice, for humankinds sin. Jesus shed his blood on the cross so we can be forgiven and become the righteousness of Christ Jesus.

Matthew 26:17– 30 NKJV The last Passover before Jesus became the lamb of God, the perfect sacrifice for our sins.

Now on the first day of the Feast of the unleavened bread the disciples came to Jesus, saying to Him, "Where do you want us to prepare for you to eat the Passover?" And He said, "Go into the city to a certain man, and say to him, 'The Teacher says, "My time is at hand; I will keep the Passover at your house with my disciples." So the disciples did as Jesus had directed them; and they prepared the Passover. And as they were eating, Jesus took bread, blessed and broke it, and gave it to the disciples and said, "take, eat; **this is my body**." Then He took the cup, and gave thanks, and gave it to them, saying, "drink from it, all of you, **for this is my blood of the <u>new covenant</u>, which is shed for many for the remission of sins**. But I say to you, I will not drink of this fruit of the vine from now on until that day when I drink it new with you in my Father's kingdom." And when they had sung a hymn, they went out to the Mount of Olives.

The Story, God's Son "Jesus Christ "

The Prayer in the Garden Luke 22: 41– 44 NKJV And he was withdrawn from them about a stone's cast, and kneeled down, and prayed, saying Father, if thou be willing, remove this cup from me: nevertheless not my Will, but thine Will be done. And there appeared an Angel unto him from heaven, strengthening him. And being in an agony he prayed more earnestly: and his sweat was as it were **great drops of blood** falling down to the ground. (Jesus **first** shedding of blood).

Jesus being flogged John 19: 1–3 NKJV Then Pilate therefore took Jesus, and the soldiers **scourged him** .The soldiers platted a **crown of thorns,** and put it on his head, and they put on him a purple robe, and said, Hail, King of the Jews, and they smote him with their hands.

This was the **second** time Jesus shedding His blood, (for by His stripes we are healed).

The Story, God's Son "Jesus Christ"

Jesus being crucified John 19:14-17 NKJV and it was the preparation of the Passover, and about the sixth hour: and he saith unto the Jews, "Behold your King". But they cried out, away with him, away with him, crucify him. Pilate saith unto them, shall I crucify your King? The chief priests answered, we have no king but Caesar. Then delivered he him therefore unto them to be crucified. And they took Jesus, and led him away. And he bearing his cross went forth into a place called the place of a skull, which is called in the Hebrew Golgotha:

And with this Jesus Christ became our Passover Lamb and perfect sacrifice for our sin. He is the only way to the Father and the Kingdom of Heaven, and eternal salvation. With this we pray, Jesus I thank you for your sacrifice on the cross. You died in my place, please forgive me my sins and save my soul. His death on the cross was **the third time** of Jesus shedding his blood, for our sins.

Jesus Christ Resurrection Matthews 28:1-5 And behold there was a great earthquake, for an Angel of the Lord descended from heaven, and came and rolled back the stone from the tomb and sat on it. His countenance was like lightening, and his clothing was as white as snow. But the Angel answered and said to the women, "don't not be afraid, for I know that you seek Jesus who was crucified. He is not here; He is risen, as He said. Come, and see the place where the Lord lay.

Who is God the Holy Spirit ?

The Holy Spirit is the third person of the Trinity. He is the presence of God the Father in the life of a spirit filled believer. The work of the Holy Spirit is to glorify Jesus Christ and make him real in the life of every believer. The Holy Spirit serves as God's divine administrator on earth. He is omniscience, omnipresence, omnipotence and eternal. The Holy Spirit is the third member of the Trinity. He is the one who gives the spiritual gifts, and empowers the believers, enabling them to proclaim the gospel of Jesus Christ. He empowers the prayers of a spirit filled believer and carries their prayers to the Father in the name of Jesus Christ. To receive the Holy Spirit, you must have accepted Jesus as your Lord and Savior. There is one God, who is Father, Son and Holy Spirit, this is the Trinity of the Godhead.

Scripture References

The third person of the Trinity (John 14:16 −18); "I (Jesus) will ask the Father, and he will give you another advocate to help you and be with you forever. The Spirit of truth, whom the world cannot receive, because it neither sees Him nor knows Him; but you know Him, for He dwells with you and will be in you. I will not leave you orphans; I will come to you, indwelling of the Father and the Son. The gospel of our salvation through Jesus Christ is sealed by the Holy Spirit (Eph.1:13 -14). In Him you also trusted, after you heard the Word of truth, the gospel of your salvation, you were sealed with the Holy Spirit of promise, who is the guarantee of our inheritance until the redemption, to the praise of His glory.

Who is God the Holy Spirit ?

The Holy Spirit is spoken of as the "Spirit of God" and the word "Spirit" in Greek meaning , "Pneuma", this means "breath" or "wind". The Holy Spirit is symbolized in the Word of God as being wind, water, fire, oil and the seal of God the Father. The Father, Son (Jesus Christ), and the Holy Spirit are linked together as one, according to **Matthew 28 :19** - "Go therefore and make disciples of all the nations, baptizing them in the name of the Father and of the Son and of the Holy Spirit.

The Spirit descended upon the Son "Jesus Christ", as a dove, as the Father's voice spoke from heaven.
 (John 14:16, 26 and 15:26; 16:7 - 13 NKJV)
The believer has access to the Father, through the Son, by the Holy Spirit. (Eph. 2:18 : 19 NKJV) For through Him (Jesus Christ), we both have access by one Spirit (the Holy Spirit), to the Father, Christ our Cornerstone. **The Holy Spirit proceeds from the Father through the Son (Jesus Christ).** (John 14:26) But the Helper, the Holy Spirit, whom the Father will send in my name, He will teach you all things, and bring to your remembrances all things that I said to you.

Scripture References

The Holy Spirit is called God (Acts 5:3-4, 1 Cor. 3:16, 12:4-6).
The Holy Spirit is eternal (Hebrews 9:14).
The Holy Spirit is omnipotent (all powerful) (Luke 1:35).

The Holy Spirit's power within Jesus and the Believer

After Jesus receives the Holy Spirit he is let by him into the Wilderness to be tempted by the devil. (Matthew 4:1-11 NKJV). Jesus speaks the Word of God to counter the devils attacks.

It is clear that Jesus spend much time with the Heavenly Father in prayer, as he walked away from his disciples to be alone. He receives the power from the Holy Spirit to heal the sick and deliver the demon possessed, multiply food and preach the gospel.

Jesus turned Water into Vine (John 2:1-11 NKJV),

Jesus multiplies five loaves of bread and two fish, feeding 5000 people. (Matthew 14:14-21,Luke 9:13-17 NKJV).

Jesus calming the storm, he commands the wind and waves to be still, and the storm immediately calms. The disciples are shocked and ask each other, "who is this man that even the wind and waves obey him? (Matthew 8:23-27, Mark 4:35-41 NKJV).

Jesus raising the dead, Jairus daughter and Lazarus and a women's son. (Luke 7:11-17, Luke 11:1- 45, Matthew 9:20- 22 NKJV).He healed and delivered many people with a many illnesses and disabilities., and casting out demons. (Matthew 9:1– 8 ; 9: 20 – 34; 12:9– 14), (Matthew 8:28– 33 ; 15: 21– 28 NKJV).

All the miracles were done by the power of the Holy Spirit dwelling in Jesus.

Chapter 1

My Encounters with the Spirit of the living God
by Cory Vosspeter

The Golden Cross

My first vision came years later when my husband and I visited the USA. Our car broke down, as we had travelled from Florida to Detroit, Michigan. It was a cold autumn evening, and we did not know where to stay or whom to call for help. We started praying for help, and within minutes, help arrived. An older woman introduced herself to me, and as I told her our situation, she offered to help. She invited us for dinner and then gave us a place to stay until my husband had repaired the car. During the night, I was given a vision; I saw a golden cross upon a hill. God's glory engulfed the cross with a radiant bright light. Suddenly, the room filled with electric energy; it flooded my being, and peace came over me. I knew everything would be alright, and God was with us; he had sent his Angels to help and protect us. God's presence came into our room and reassured me that God's hand was upon us.

Receiving a new language

My husband and I fulfilled a life long dream and flew to North America to travel. My husband could speak a little bit English and so we could get by. One day I had to go to the store to buy eggs, what I didn't know was, that they sold hard boiled eggs. I couldn't read the english language, so I just bought the eggs. When I arrived at our little rented apartment, I tried to crack the shell in order to fry the eggs, but to my surprise they were hard boiled eggs. I also bought full cream, instead of milk for our cereal. When my husband joined a group of people to visit a tourist attraction, I was left alone. At the pool, some children tried to communicate with me, but I only spoke German. I couldn't understand what they were saying. I was quite sad because, I couldn't understand their language. I was not able to read and write english either. Then, just before we went to bed, I prayed to my heavenly Father. I said Father God please give me the english language supernaturally tonight. When I wake up I will understand this language, read, write, and speak it. Then we went to bed, in the morning when I awoke, I switched the TV on. I noticed then, that I could understand what was spoken. I grabbed the newspaper and I could read what was written. And I read out loud and noticed that I spoke perfectly english. God blessed me with this gift for a time as this, to write this book and to reveal the spirit realm to all. I have no problem to understand different dialects of the english language either.

John 14:13-17 NKJV And whatever you *ask* in My name, that I will do, that the Father may be glorified in the Son. If you *ask anything* in My name, I will do it

The Music Box

On a nice warm autumn day, my husband, a friend, and I drove out to Point Peele in Ontario, Canada. This is the southern tip of Canada and a forty five minute drive from Windsor. As we were walking at the beach, God spoke to me and said to me, "Go a bit further up to the right; I have something for you." As I walked along the beach, I wondered what it could be. Then, I saw a little white Nativity Music box standing in the sand. I picked it up and thanked the Lord for His great gift. With this gift, God confirmed to me that the virgin birth was true. He had sent His son to earth, to die in your place.

The music box plays the song; "Silent Night, Holy Night."

Protection and Intervention

I was about eight months pregnant and living in Windsor, Ontario, Canada. In the evening I got a craving for chocolate milk, I had to cross a busy road in front of our house. As I walked up to the pedestrian light, God said to me, be careful a car will run the red light. I prayed right away for protection and crossed the road. On the way back as I was about to cross the road again, waiting for the pedestrian light to switch to green, it was then when I found myself being translated to the middle of the road. I came too, as a cold wind blew on my hair, shooting past me was the car that had ran the red light. An Angel must had moved me to the middle of the road. Shocked, I crossed the rest of the road, praising God for his protection.

(Psalms 91)

A Heavenly Experience

On the day our son Jacob was born, I had one sharp pain in my back, and was told by the Lord that it was time to go to the hospital. In the hospital I found out that our baby boy was in a breach position, and I would have an Caesarean birth. As they placed the anaesthetic in, something went wrong, and I found myself leaving my body. I remember traveling through a tunnel of light, and all of the sudden stood face to face with Jesus. I knew I was in spirit form, but felt like myself. The glory that emanated from Jesus, engulfed my being. I felt the most amazing peace, as love flooded my spirit body. I did not want to leave heaven, but Jesus told me that I had to go back for Jacobs's sake. I returned to my body, and all of the sudden felt the pain, and the heaviness of the earthly realm. I cried out for Jesus as I couldn't see him anymore. Just then I felt the nurse touching my face, and hearing her voice, calling for me to wake up. My recovery was short as my body healed fast; I praised God.

The Crown of Thorns

We visited the Vineyard Church in Toronto, Canada, as we entered, an overwhelming peace came over me. During the worship service, in a vision, I saw the crown of thorns sitting on my head. I felt something dripping down my head and onto my face. I touched my face but couldn't see anything. In a vision, I saw Jesus wearing the crown of thorns, and blood was dripping down his face and onto his beard. God was affirming to me that Jesus is the Messiah and son of God. Later in the evening, I wondered why people were laughing and rolling around on the floor.

I said to my husband, surely this can't be of God; the people are acting crazy. On the way to our car, an energy suddenly hit me right into my stomach area, and my hands started to burn. It felt as if tiny flames were flickering in the palms of my hands. Joy came over me, and I began to laugh uncontrollably. The invisible flames stayed in the palms of my hands, and I went to sleep with them. Later that night, I was awakened by a bubbling sensation in my chest. I sat up, and this fire took hold of my tongue and head. My friends said that this was the baptism of the Holy Spirit and to pray. As I started to pray, an unknown language came forth, and after an hour of praying , it stopped. This was the baptism of the Holy Spirit.

The Wooden carving at the beach

In 2005 my second husband had moved my son and I from Canada to New Zealand. I had a really hard time; the culture was very different here. I prayed to the Lord to confirm, if this was his Will for us to be living in Canada or in New Zealand. I was very conflicted and had a hard time with my decision. Couple days had past, and as we walked along the beach, I found a small round wooden carving. On one side of the round wooden medallion was, the Maple Leaf and it read "Canada", and on the other side was a Koru and it read, "New Zealand". In a time where I was so conflicted, God had spoken to me again through a sign. It was my decision in which country I wanted to live. Later on, a prophetic word was given to me; "You are blessed in Canada and out of Canada".

Chapter 2

Encounters with the Angels of God
By Cory Vosspeter

"Salvation"

Growing up in Germany, I encountered the supernatural from a very early age on. At the age of three, I started seeing the spiritual world that was around me. Growing up, I had too many questions and not enough answers. I started reading books that dealt with the supernatural, seeking answers to my questions, why was I seeing evil spirits? On some occasion they would physically attack me. I did not know what to do, so I turned to the only place which I knew, the Catholic Church. As I explained to the priest what had happened, he told me that there was no hell, and no devil, and sent me away. A few month's had passed, and I heard a knock on our apartment door. As I opened the door, I found an older man with a bible in his hand standing there. Before I could ask why he had come, the man said, "Cory, you are having a problem, can I come in?". I replied, "who are you, and how do you know my name?" I said, I don't have a problem, and closed the door in front of him. As I was moving away from the door, I suddenly felt some static electricity and heat on the right side of my upper body and head. An unseen hand touched my right shoulder. I heard an audible voice near my right ear saying to me, "Cory" open the door right now; you know you are having a problem with the demonic forces." Waves of electricity and heat engulfed my body. Now shaken, I opened the door and found the older man still standing there. The man asked again if he could come in, and then said he was an Angel sent to me by God. He explained that Satan had partitioned for my life and wanted me dead. The Angel explained that the next day, when I had tried to cross the busy road in front of our house, a truck would have taken my life, and I would have died and gone to hell. I thought, was he truly an Angel sent by God?

Now, in shock, tears were streaming down my face, and for some minutes, I sat silently, thinking if this could be true. Was the older man just from some religious organization? The Angel could hear my thoughts and answered me, saying he was an Angel sent by God and was speaking the truth. I cried and said, I don't want to die and go to hell. He opened the Word of God and started reading to me from John 3:16: "For God so loved the world that He gave his only begotten son." The Angel asks me if I want to give my life into the hands of God, and accept the sacrifice Jesus Christ had provided. I replied, yes and with this, we prayed, "Jesus, please forgive me my sins; come into my life I want to live for you." Father, take my life into your hands from this day forward in the name of Jesus Christ, I pray." The Angel said to throw all spiritual and New Age books that were in my possession, in the rubbish bin. He said those books were open gateways for the enemy to enter once life. The books had opened doors to the demonic realm and given the demonic forces the legal right to be in my life and our home. He said these spiritual books sow deception and are against God's Will for humankind. He urged me also to stop watching horror movies, as they are open gateways to the demonic realm. I was shocked that the Angel knew I had such books in my house. With the Angel still present, I threw all books that contained the teachings and knowledge of ghosts, hauntings, and such alike, in the outside trash bin. We said our good-byes, and he reminded me that if I felt an evil presence standing behind me or some demonic force in our home, I should call upon Emmanuel, which means God with us. With this said, he left our house. After a few seconds, I opened the door but the Angel was gone.

."Testing"

We were now living in Canada, and as I was drinking my morning coffee, heard the voice of the Lord saying to me, "Get up and walk to the grocery store." I was surprised but got up and put my shoes on. I thought to myself, this could get interesting. The way to the grocery store would take me over a small bridge, and it was about a twenty minute walk. As I walked, an African American man suddenly stood before me, asking me where the nearest grocery store was. I gave the man directions, and for a split second, I turned away as I heard my name being called. I couldn't see anyone, and I turned back towards the man. To my surprise, he was gone; I wondered where he could have walked off so quickly, no bus or car had stopped. Standing on top of the bridge now, I had a view over the area, and the man was nowhere to be seen. As I walked on for a little while longer, I arrived at the grocery store. To my surprise, the man was waiting there. As I approached the supermarket's entry, the man asked me, "do you know Jesus Christ"? I was startled and said, "yes, I know him personally; he is my best friend." He then said to me, "tell me about Jesus Christ, who is he?" I proceeded to tell him about Jesus, that he had died for the sins of humanity, so none would perish and go to hell. The man answered," you have passed the test, which God the Father has given you." "You have not denied his son Jesus Christ, and neither shall the Father deny you." I understood that this man was not human but an Angel of the most high God. After he said this, he spoke a blessings over me, and walked down the sidewalk. As I watched him walking off, he became less and less visible until he disappeared before my eyes into thin air.

Scripture References: Exodus 20:20 - "Moses said to the people, "Do not fear; for God has come to test you. **Job 23:10** - "He knows the way that I take; When

Angel of Protection at the Bridal Vail Falls

My son and our student from China visited the Bridal Vail Falls near Raglan, New Zealand. It was pretty late in the day when we arrived there. Both young men walked the steps down to the bottom of the Falls. I chose to wait on the top at the Falls, looking down and enjoying the view. I must have waited about a half hour for both of them to make their way back up. The sun was setting, I called out to them, to hurry back up. I heard noises coming from the Forest, I felt a evil presence and being watched from within the Forest. An uneasy feeling and fear came over me, I started praying for protection. I was alone and there and no other people were at the Falls anymore. I called out to my son again, as I couldn't see him. All of the sudden a young man walked around the corner, he said to me; "don't be afraid, I go and get the boys." They are for sure on the way back up and be here soon. I looked at the young man startled, but thanked him. He went down the path to the stairs that led to the bottom of the Falls. Soon after that, my son and the student came to me. I said, did you guys see a young man; did he tell you that I am waiting for you? And my son said, yes, the young man had told them to hurry back, and he went down the stairs that led to the bottom of the Falls. There is no other way out but to walk back up the stairs and out through the Forest and to the carpark. We walked the ten-minute walk through the Forest, back to the carpark. By the time we reached our car, it was quiet dark already. I noticed that there was no other car in the carpark. We waited another 30 minutes in our car, for the man to return from the Bridal Vail Falls. But he didn't return, it was then that I realized that he must been an Angel of protection.

The Angels at the Gardens

At a cloudy November day in 2011 my son and I visited the Hamilton Gardens. We visited the Italian Renaissance Garden when, I felt being watched. I turned around but couldn't see anyone. I took a photo and to my amazement, Gods Guardian Angels had opened a dimensional portal, in form of a golden gate.

This photo is before the golden gate appeared.

The Angels at the Gardens

This is the photo with the golden gate and the Angles visible.

The Angels at the Gardens

This is the photo with the golden gate and the Angles visible.

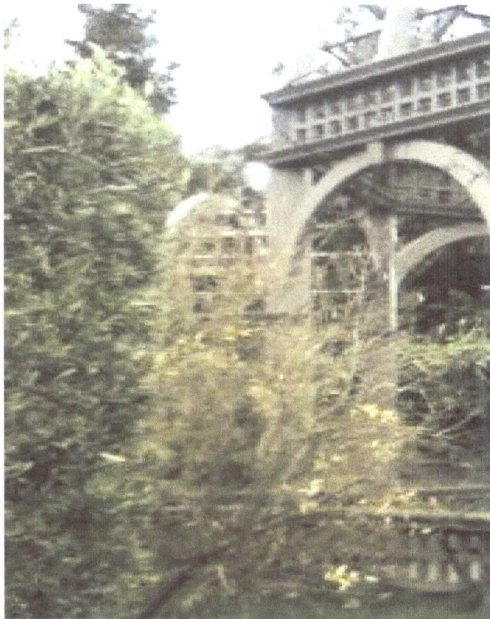

The Angels in the Rainbow

I photographed these Angels after a heavy rainstorm, the Angels looking down on the Town of Whakatane New Zealand.

Whakatane New Zealand 2008

Scripture Reference NKJV Palms 91:11 "For He will command his Angels to concerning you to protect you all your ways. They shall bear thee up in their hands, lest thou dash they foot against a stone."

Angel in the clouds

At the end of a nice day at the Ski field on Mt. Ruapehu, I noticed this beautiful Angel in the Sky.

Taupo New Zealand 2009
(Enhanced)

Scripture References NKJV Luke 4:10 - For it is written: He will give His angels orders concerning you, to protect you.

Hebrews 1:14 "Angels are "servants" spirits sent to care for people who will inherit salvation."

Proverbs 15:3 "The eyes of the LORD are in every place, watching the evil and the good."

1 Peter 3:12 "For the eyes of the LORD are towards the righteous, and His ears attend to their prayers, but the face of the LORD is against those who do evil."

Colossians 1:16 " For by him were all things created, that are in heaven, and that are in earth, visible and invisible, whether they be thrones, or dominions, or principalities, or powers: all things were created by him, and for him."

Angelic Face in the Sky

My sons class went on a field trip, as I was taking photos of the children, we noticed this face in the sky.

Rotorua New Zealand 2009
(Enhanced)

Scripture References NKJV

Psalms 33:18 "The eyes of the LORD are toward the righteous and His ears are open to their cry."

Psalms 91:11 " For He shall give His angels charge over you, to keep you in all your ways.

Angel of God clothed with a rainbow and demonic spirit.

We had just visited Raglan and were driving back to Hamilton, I noticed the Angel dressed with a rainbow, and what looks like a demonic entity in the sky.

Hamilton (Raglan) New Zealand 2014
(Enhanced)

Scripture Reference NKJV

Revelation 10:1 "I saw still another mighty Angel coming down from heaven, clothed with a cloud. And a rainbow was on his head, his face was like the sun, and his feet like pillars of fire."

Ephesians 6:12 "For we do not wrestle against flesh and blood, but against principalities, against powers, against the ruler of the darkness of this age, against

Where do Angels originate from?

God the Supreme Being is the creator of all living things. We read in the Word of God, he created the seen and unseen realm, on earth and in the heavens. The scriptures reveal to us that God has an everlasting kingdom, and in his kingdom, there are created beings called Angels. The Angels of God are commanded to watch over mankind, to protect the human race from the attacks of the dark forces, the fallen angels (more about them in chapter 2). The Hebrew word for Angel is "Malak" meaning "a messenger", therefore the angels of God are messengers. In the Word of God there are many examples of Angels bringing massages from God to humankind, both in the old as well as in the New Testament of the Word of God.

Scripture references: (NKJV)

Colossians 1:16 - 17(16) For by him were all things created, that are in heaven, and that are in earth, visible and invisible, whether they be thrones, or dominions, or principalities, or powers: all things were created by him, and for him: (17) And he (God) is before all things, and by him all things consist. Nehemiah 9: 6 (6) Thou, even thou, art LORD alone; thou hast made heaven. The heaven of heavens, with all their host, the earth, and all things that are therein, the seas, and all that is therein, and thou preserve them all; and the hosts of heaven worship thee. Psalms 148:1-2 God himself created the Angels and other heavenly hosts. (1) Praise ye the LORD, praise ye the LORD from the heavens; praise him in the heights. (2) Praise ye him, all his Angels: praise ye him, all his hosts.

Scripture reference human encounters with Gods messengers (to name a few)

Genesis 18:1-33 Abraham and wife (1) And the LORD appeared unto him in the plains of Mamre: and he sat in the tent door in the heat of the day;**(2) t**he lift up his eyes and looked, and, lo, three men stood by him: and when he saw [them], he ran to meet them from the tent door, and bowed himself toward the ground. **Genesis 19:1-38 Lot and his family (1)** And there came two Angels to Sodom at even; and Lot sat in the gate of Sodom: and Lot seeing [them] rose up to meet them; and he bowed himself with his face toward the ground; **Luke 1:1-25 a priest named Zacharias (11-13)** And there appeared unto him an Angel of the Lord standing on the right side of the altar of incense. And when Zacharias saw [him], he was troubled, and fear fell upon him. But the Angel said unto him, fear not, Zacharias: for thy prayer is heard; and thy wife Elisabeth shall bear thee a son, and thou shall call his name John. **(18-19)** And Zacharias said to the Angel, how shall I know this, for I am an old man, and my wife well stricken in years? And the Angel answering said unto him, I am Gabriel that stand in the presence of God; and am sent to speak unto you and to show you these glad tidings.

What are Angels?

Angels have free Will to choose ("the fallen angels"). We read in the Word of God, Angels are sprit beings; they are ministering spirits. Because they are spirit beings, they are not limited to the physical realm like we humans are. The Angels have real personalities, intelligence and will. Angels are not omnipresent like God is, but they are invisible to the human eyes. When directed by God Angels can take on human form to help humankind, and then they become mediators between God and men. God and the Angels are immortal; they are not subject to physical death. When God created the Angels, he gave them free will, meaning they do have the power of choice to obey or disobey God. Just like mankind was given free Will by God to choose, whom he will serve. Lucifer the Arch Angel, who chose to disobey God, is one example that Angels do have free Will. Angels are messengers bringing warnings, judgement, protect, comfort, help and heal. The Word of God gives reference of a whole range of ministering spirits. The Angels are the sons of God, created spiritual beings such as Cherubim, Seraphim, and the Archangels. Throughout Revelation we read that the Angels of God bringing judgement upon the earth.

In **Luke 2: 8 – 14** *The Angels bringing a message of Jesus birth to the Shepherds.*

<u>Scripture references:</u>

In Acts 12: 7- 9 The Angel of the Lord protects, helps and brings messages. The night before Herod was to bring him to trial, Peter was sleeping between two soldiers, bound with two chains, and sentries stood guard at the entrance. **(7)** Suddenly an Angel of the Lord appeared and a light shone in the cell. He struck Peter on the side and woke him up. "Quick, get up!" he said, and the chains fell off Peter's wrists. **(8)** Then the Angel said to him "Put on your clothes and sandals." And Peter did so. "Wrap your cloak around you and follow me," the angel told him. him out of the prison, but he had no idea that what the Angel was doing was really happening; he thought he was seeing a vision.

The Cherubim Angel's

Cherubim Angels are to worship God and protect his glory. Cherubim Angels having wings, two of such Cherubim where mounted on the Arch of God.

<u>Scripture References:</u> **Geneses 3: 24** after he drove the man out, he placed on the east side of the Garden of Eden Cherubim and a flaming sword flashing back and forth to guard the way to the tree of life. **Exodus 25: 17** "Make an atonement cover of pure gold—two and a half cubits long and a cubit and a half wide. **(18)** And make two Cherubim out of hammered gold at the ends of the cover. **(19)** Make one Cherub on one end and the second Cherub on the other; make the Cherubim of one piece with the Arch of Covenant. **Revelation 4:6–9, 6** also before the throne there was what looked like a sea of glass, clear as crystal.

The Seraphim Angels

In the word of God, the Seraphim Angels are described as having six wings. The Seraphim are focused on worshipping God.

Scripture References: **Isaiah 6: 1-7 (6)** in the year that King Uzziah died, I saw the Lord seated on a throne, high and exalted, and the train of his robe filled the temple. Above him were Seraphs, each with six wings: with two wings they covered their faces, with two they covered their feet. **Isaiah 6: 2-4 (2)** above him were Seraphs, each with six wings: With two wings they covered their faces, with two they covered their feet, and with two they were flying. **(3)** And they were calling to one another: "Holy, holy, holy is the LORD Almighty; the whole earth is full of his glory.

What are Arch Angels?

Arch Angels are the protectors of humankind, the Word of God speaks of numerous Angles. In **Daniel 12:1** we read that; Arch Angel Michael is the protector of the people. *(12) "At that time Michael, the great prince who protects your people, will arise. There will be a time of distress such as has not happened from the beginning of nations until then. But at that time your people—everyone whose name is found written in the book—will be delivered.*

Other Scripture references: Daniel 10: 13 and 21, 1Thessalonians 44:16.

What do Angels look like ?

What do Angels look like, that is the question many people have asked over time. In the Word of God, Angels are explained as spirit beings. The angels have been known to visit us in human form. In this book I will show you what the Angels of God look like. Under the guidance of the Holy Spirit I have taken pictures of these angelic beings. God is revealing to humankind the reality of the heavenly realm and his holy Angels, but also the reality of Hades (Hell) and its evil spirits and demons. But let's see what the Word of God say's, what Angels look like?

Scripture references: **NIV and NKJV Bible.**

Matthews 28: 3 - His countenance was like lightning, and his raiment white as snow.

Luke 2: 8 – 14 8 and there were Shepherds living out in the fields near-by, keeping watch over their flocks at night. [9] and the Angel of the Lord appeared to them and the glory of the Lord shone around them, and they were terrified. **Genesis 18 and 19** we read that the Angel of the Lord sat down with Abraham and eat. Angels are known to come and talk to humankind in a normal human form and human body, looking like you and me. The Word of God is clear and it say's in the Word of God, watch who you might entertain. Angels are mentioned at least 108 times in the Old Testament and 165 times in the New Testament.

Chapter 3

The reality of the demonic spirits
by Cory Vosspeter

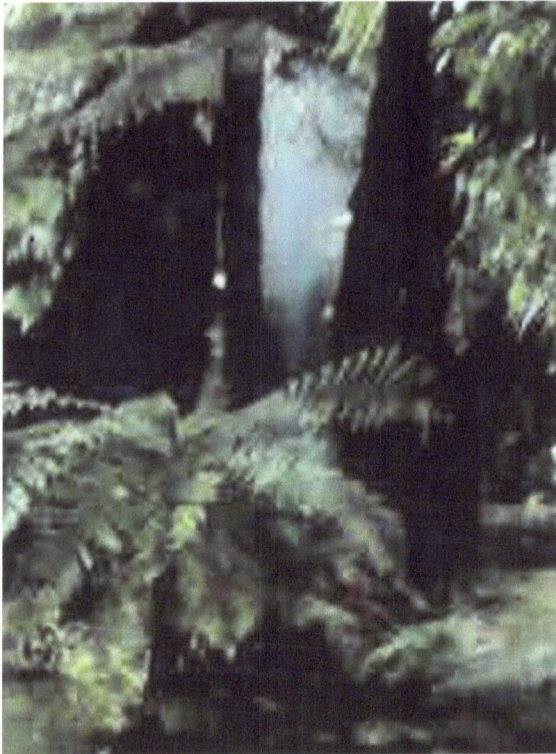

At a popular tourist attraction this spirit was watching us.

Evil spirits hiding in plain sight

I did not know that evil spirits can come in many form and sizes. Some are very small, and dressed in pants, jackets and hats. They enter our dimension freely and unnoticed and hidden from our human eyes. The people that lived in this house, moved to Hamilton in 2010. After couple month living in their rental property, grotesque faces would appear, imprinted into the fabric of the carpet. We were invited to anointed the house, commanding the spirits to leave. But nothing worked, in the end, the people moved out of their house. It was then that they learned, that the house was built on unclean grounds. After I had taken photos, I noticed that an evil spirit was sitting under their table. I believe that this spirit had caused all the faces to appear on their carpet.

Spirits walking among us

This spirit is wearing a long coat and a cone hat, as he is walking towards a dimensional gateway. He is in spirit form.

My experience with the demonic spirits in New Zealand

We took a shortcut through the forest on the way home from a day at Mount Ruapehu skiing. As we drove on, we saw what looked like a tall figure with a weird hat and a long black coat standing at the side of the forest road. The Lord said, "Switch the truck into four-wheel drive." I immediately obeyed, when all of the sudden, the left-hand back tire popped, and we had to pull over. I looked in the mirror out of the back window and couldn't see the man anymore. I was wondering if it was the reaper or a demon of death that wanted to harm us. The sun was setting, and we had to change the tire in the middle of the forest. As my husband got to work, I told my son to stay in the truck, and I started praying and keeping watch. I could feel the evil lurking in the forest. I had never felt something like it. Growls could be heard from behind the trees. I encouraged my husband to please hurry up, as I felt unsafe. We were glad when the tire was changed, and we could drive on. After a twenty minute drive, we reached the Kawerau Hydro Dam. After this experience, I refused to take the shortcut through the forest.

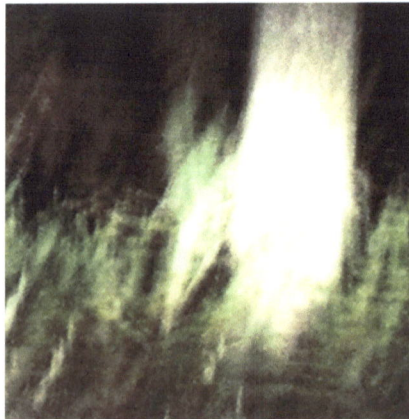

Evil at the Rotorua Hot Springs

Sometimes evil spirits using the mist to manifest. In this photo two demonic spirits manifesting through the mist at this hot spring.

Spiritual House cleansing

In 2012 we were invited to a church members home, to bless the house and pray with the occupants. Their twenty-six-year-old son was hearing voices that were telling him to kill himself. The doctors had given him medication to quiet the voices in his head. When we entered the house, I noticed many Buddha statues. The family brought these souvenirs back from their last holiday. It was then that after couple of weeks their son started hearing voices. After we had gotten rid of these statures (Idols), we prayed and blessed the house and occupants. I took photos, and will share them here with you. Demon spirits are hidden in plain sight at this Buddha statue.

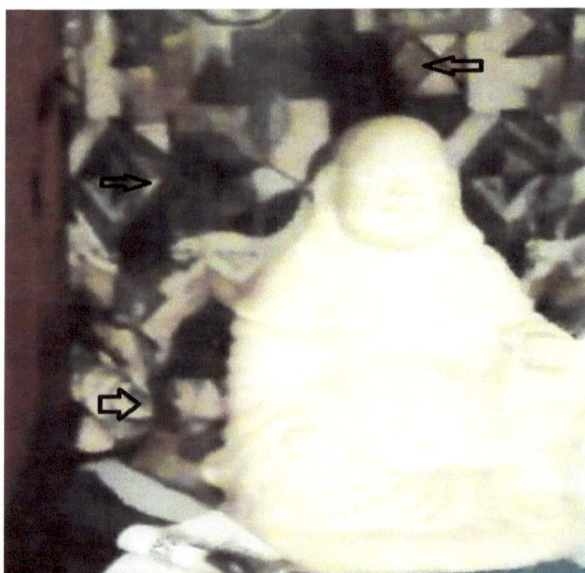

Spiritual House cleansing

The little Imp demon standing on the kitchen counter whispering bad thoughts of suicide into his victim's ear.

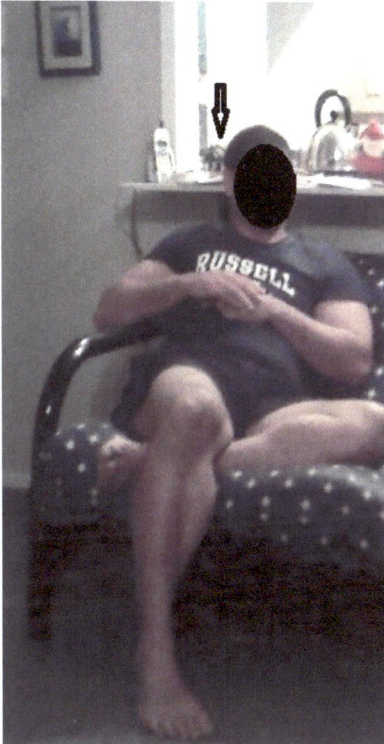

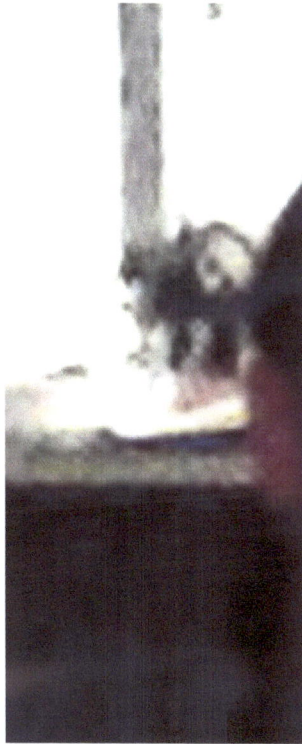

The Waterfall at the Gorge and it's spirits

Again I had a dream of a waterfall that was in a hidden place, near a busy road. After much research I found the hidden sight and our prayer team and I set out on a journey. After a long drive we arrived at the sight. I took photos before and after we had prayed. This is the photo after the prayer, the Vail that separates our world and theirs has been pulled away for a split second. Here we see a man's face and what looks like a woman and child's face in the waterfall.

Evil at the Lake

After an early morning prayer and time spend with the Lord, He told me to go outside and photograph the lake at the campground. When I came near the water, the mist moved away from me. The Lord told me to take photos, I did so.

These are the original photos

Evil at the Lake

The demonic spirits at this popular campground, are manifesting where children play. Here we see the evil spirit that is manifesting in the morning mist on the campground lake. (Spirits in the mist)

Evil at the Lake

Ghostly encounter at Fairy Springs in Rotorua

The reality of the demonic realm
by Cory Vosspeter

<u>These are examples that open doors to the demonic realm.</u>

Demonic doorways are opened through Idol worship, places that were dedicated to Idols, demons and evil spirits.

Places where blood had been spilled, through murder and blood sacrifices through Occult practices.

Reading New Age and other spiritual books, watching horror movies, martial art practices, yoga practises and alike.

Tarot card reading, Ouija board, Dungeons and Dragons game, and alike, and taking drugs. Having Idols in your house, like Buddha statues pictures of foreign god's and alike, and the believe in crystal and spirit healing, will invite evil spirits and demons into the house.

"Biblical scripture references"

Demonic spirits and their nature:

The Word of God describes many kinds of demonic spirits that are under satanic control. There are many different demonic spirits have different assignments. Demons are morally evil in character and wickedness. **(Matthew 12:22-30).**

Genesis 4:10 - "The voice of your brother's blood is crying to me from the ground.

Exodus 20:3 - 5 - "You shall have no other gods before Me. "You shall not make for yourself a carved image, any likeness of anything that is in heaven above, or that is in the earth beneath, or that is in the water under the earth. You shall not bow down to them nor serve them. For I, the Lord your God, am a jealous God, visiting the Iniquity of the fathers upon the children to the third and fourth generation of those who hate Me.

Isaiah 45:20 - Who carry the wood of their carved image, and pray to a god that cannot save.

Deuteronomy 18:9 - 11 - You shall not learn to follow the abomination of those nations. There shall not be found among you anyone who makes his son or his daughter pass through the fire. Nor one who practices witchcraft, or a soothsayer, or one who interprets omens, or a sorcerer. Nor one who conjures spells, or medium, or a spiritist, or one who calls up the dead.

Demonic spirits (to name a few).

Unclean spirits - Luke 11:24 - 26 What happens when an **unclean spirit** returns after being cast out of a person? "When an unclean spirit goes out of a man, he goes through dry places, seeking rest; and finding none, he says; "I will return to my house from which I came." And when he comes, he finds it swept and put in order. Then he goes and takes with him seven other spirits more wicked than himself, and they enter and dwell there; and the last state of that man (person) is worse than before it got cast out.

Spirit of Infirmity - Luke 13:11 - 13 And behold, there was a woman who had a **spirit of infirmity** for eighteen years, and was bent over and could in no way raise herself up. But when Jesus saw her, He called her to him and said to her," women, you are loosed from your infirmity. And He laid His hands on her, and immediately she was made straight, and glorified God.

Seducing spirits - 1 Timothy 4 :1 - 4 The Great Apostasy. Now the Holy Spirit expressly says, that in latter times some will depart from the faith, giving heed to deceiving spirits and doctrines of demons, speaking lies in hypocrisy, having their own conscience seared with a hot iron, forbidding to marry, and commanding to abstain from foods which God created to be received with thanksgiving by those who believe and know the truth. For every creature of God is good, and nothing is to be refused if it is received with thanksgiving.

Demonic spirits (to name a few).

Familiar spirits - 1 Samuel 28:7 - 25 Then Saul said to his servants; "find me a woman who is a medium, that I may go to her and inquire of her." And his servants said to him; "in fact, there is a woman who is a medium at En Dor." In the end, God's judgement falls on Saul for going to a medium.

Divination spirit - Acts 16:16 - 19 Now it happened, as we went to prayer, that a certain slave girl possessed with a spirit of divination met us, who brought her masters much profit by fortune telling.

Evil spirits - Luke 8:2 - and certain women who had been healed of evil spirits and infirmities. **Acts 19:12** - So that even handkerchiefs or aprons were brought from his body to the sick, and the diseases left them and the evil spirits went out of them. (**Judges 9:23, 1Samuel 16:14,23, Luke 7:21, 8:2, Matthew 15:22**)

Scripture Reference:

Zechariah 10:2 - For the idol's delusion; the diviners envision lies and tell false dreams; they comfort in vain. Therefore, the people went their way like sheep; they were in trouble because there was no shepherd.

Galatians 5:19-21- The acts of the flesh are evident: sexual immorality, impurity and debauchery; Idolatry and witchcraft; hatred, discord, jealousy, fits of rage, selfish ambition, dissensions, factions: and envy, drunkenness, orgies, and the like. As I did before, I warn you that those who live like this will not inherit the Kingdom of God.

Those sins lead to spiritual death and eternity in hell, being separated from a loving heavenly Father.

Psalms 135:15-18 - The nations' idols are silver and gold, made by human hands. They have a mouth but cannot speak and eyes but cannot see. They have ears but cannot hear, nor is there breath in their mouths. Those who make them will be like them, and so will all who trust them.

Isaiah 45:20 - Gather together and come; assemble, you fugitives from the nations, ignorant are those who carry about idols of wood, who pray to gods that cannot save.

End-time warning through visitations, dreams and

visions

by Cory Vosspeter

End-time warning through dreams and visions
by Cory Vosspeter

The first encounter with God and end time warning came in June 1995, when my husband and I were housesitting for a friend in Windsor, Ontario, Canada. Reading the newspaper on a Saturday morning, I ask the Lord, " who is this Prophet Muhammed"? The Lord spoke to me immediately, saying that Prophet Muhammed was a misled Prophet whom the enemy had deceived. He said the angel of light, "Satan," deceived many. Then, suddenly, the atmosphere in the living room changed; it became electric, and a brilliant bluish-white light filled the room. Warms and electricity flooded my body. I closed my eyes due to the brilliant light in the room. Suddenly, I heard the Father God speak from the direction of the balcony door. He said that if I sent my son Jesus to the earth right now, two-third of all the people would perish and go to hell. I was shocked; the fear of God gripped me, and I started pleading for the people's lives. I said, "Please, Father, delay; we are not ready; the Church is not ready; oh God, delay the judgment for mankind's sake." The Father responded to my plea; he said, "I will delay a little while longer," and with this, He vanished. I was physically shaken and felt like Moses did, pleading with God not to destroy the Children of Israel.

I apologize to our Muslim brothers for any offence this may have caused. This said, it is better to know the truth than to burn in hell for all eternity.

End-time warning through dreams and visions
by Cory Vosspeter

In July 2025 an Angel of the Lord visited me in a vision, he said warn my people, Jesus is returning soon, the Angels getting ready to sound the trumpets. Then in the vision, in an instance Jesus was here on earth walking the street towards a church. He entered and found the Pastor asleep at his desk. Jesus woke the Pastor up, in shock the Pastor looked at Jesus and said; "Lord what are you doing here, we are not expecting you for a long time." The Lord is coming for His church before the great tribulation, the wrath of God that comes upon the earth. It is time to repent and to get ready, as our home is not on earth, but our home is with our Lord Jesus Christ in heaven.

1Thessalonians 5:2 - For yourselves are fully aware that the day of the Lord will come like a thief in the night.

Matthew 24: 43 - But know this, that if the master of the house had known in what part of the night the thief was coming, he would have stayed awake and would not let his house be broken into.

Revelation 16: 15 - Behold, I am coming like a thief. Blessed is the one who stays awake, keeping his garments on, that he may not go about naked and be seen exposed.

Warning Dreams and visions
By Cory Vosspeter

I had three dreams that started with the first warning dream on the **28th of June, 2005**. But two more warning dreams would follow on the exact dates, **28th June 2009 and 28th June 2010.**

In a vision He showed me a coastal city, an earthquake was about to happen. It was early morning, children were dropped off at school, and people were on the way to work. All of the sudden the earth started to shake violently. The Angel said, here **the sun, moon and stars won't give their light.** Again, the Angel said, "warn my people, if they don't listen, they will perish with the wicked."

In the first two dreams (28th June 2005 and 2009), I was told to warn His people of the upcoming judgements that the Lord God would sent to earth. In all three dreams, an Angel of the Lord appeared to me, warning me of a tsunami that was triggered by an undersea earthquake and volcanic eruptions. I saw whole coastal cities disappearing beneath the waves. Whales were now swimming where once people had lived and worked.

The third and final warning dream from 28th of June 2010.

Once again, the same Angel appeared to me, urging me to warn the people, of the upcoming judgements. He said; " **warn my people**, for now, the judgement of God draws near." A tsunami mankind has not experienced yet is coming, and many people will perish. He said, go and warn my people, the Father had enough from the wickedness that is on the earth. He said; "they are *lovers of money*, *lovers off materialistic things*, and lovers *of self*. They are *Idol worshippers* and they do not believe and do not repent. After I had warned the people and surely they didn't listen and mocked me. Then the Angel appeared in front of me and said to me; "come it is time to go". He stretched his hand forth. I grabbed his hand and He took me high up above the earth. As I looked back, I said to the Angel; " what about all the children, they are the innocent?". The Angel answered me saying; "the Father God had enough off the wickedness and the sins of the people, He will send judgement now to the earth." I knew instantly what was to come, sadness gripped me, thinking of all the people that would perish now.

In 2007, I warned many pastors and churches and people, as the Lord directed me, but none thought that God would bring destruction and judgement. Now the times getting darker, and we know the Wormwood/Apophis makes a very close fly by on the 13th April 2029. Could this be the judgement of God that the Angel had warned about? What would happen when this Asteroid would strike in the Pacific Ocean, or brake up in our atmosphere? We can read this in **Revelation 8:7–13.** *Read what would happen, when such an Asteroid would brake up during entry and one part hits the ocean and other parts strike the land. I hope people repent and turn from their wicked ways, before it is too late.*

This ghostly figure of a man is pointing out to sea.

The next day the Lord told me to drive out to Whakatane Heads area, that is in the Bay of Plenty of New Zealand. It was early morning, when I arrived there, and saw a ghostly figure of a man standing on top of the cliff that is above the city, he was pointing out to sea. Was this another conformation?

"Another Conformation"

Days had past when He <u>confirmed</u> the dream in my time of prayer. The following day as I walked my son to school, I noticed some strange cloud formations in the sky. Walking on, I heard the voice of the Lord urging me to take a photo. I only had my cellphone with me, which was the Samsung Envy at that time, and took this photo. God is spirit, therefore this photo is not as clear. I do believe this to be an end time message and prophetic warning, to us all. I wondered if the women laying on a pillow was a representation of the sleeping Church. On the left upper side of the picture is a **white horse**. In the middle we see an Angel, and in the middle of the Angel, the face of Jesus Christ. On the side of the Angel, the eyes of God, and more.

Original photo ——————————— Contrast added

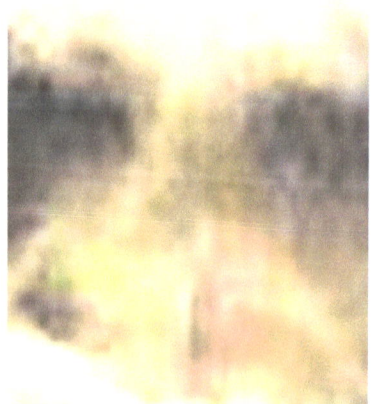

"Another Conformation"

Vision

The last warning came in **February 2011**, while we lived in Hamilton, New Zealand, I received an **open vision**. I was standing in the kitchen washing dishes, and looking out of the kitchen window into our backyard. Suddenly, our kitchen window became a TV screen, I saw what looked like a huge fireball coming towards our house. As it flew over our house, the earth started to shake wildly. I held unto the sink as I felt the shaking and thought it was an earthquake. In the vision, I saw that the flaming rock landing in a wooden area filled with pine trees, and now everything was on fire. People were running for their lives. Then, the vision all of the sudden stopped. I was shaken and asked the Lord what I had seen. The Lord answered me and said, "Wormwood". I knew the Wormwood prophecy that is found in **Revelation 8: 7– 13 "The first four trumpets of Judgement"**

Conformation

In 2023, As I watched the Sid Roth show, the guest speaker was a Prophet named "Tom Horn." As I watched the show, Tom Horn shared his dream of an Asteroid called Apophis that, in his dream, had hit the earth. I was stunned to learn that another Prophet had received the warning of an Asteroid striking the Earth, as I had. Now, all my dreams and visions made sense, if this Asteroid would strike the earth, everything I had seen will come to pass. When Apophis comes closer to earth, earthquakes would multiply, and volcanoes would erupt. If it breaks apart at entry and hits the earth and the sea, earthquakes, volcanic eruptions, wildfires, and a vast tsunami waves would destroy our world. Is this the judgement of God that the Angel had warned me about? (Read Revelation 8)

Update: July 31, 2025 Article - The Scientific community witnessed a significant development when astronomers from the European Space Agency revealed potential impact zones for asteroid 2023DW. This massive space rock, classified as a "city killer." could potentially strike Earth in 2032. The highest probability impact location has been identified in the South Pacific Ocean, approximately 1,500 kilometres east of New Zealand.

After this I have received a scripture reference.

Zechariah 13:8-9 " And it shall come to pass in all the land, says the Lord, that two -thirds in it shall be cut off and die, but one-third shall be left in it. I will bring the one -third through the fire, refine them as silver is refined, and test them as gold is tested. They will call me by my name, and I will answer them. I will say, "This are my people, and each one will say, "The Lord is my God."

Ending Words

If this Asteroid 2023DW would hit the South Pacific all what the Angel said would come to pass. Earthquakes, volcanic eruptions and a tsunami so powerful which mankind had never experienced would hit the coast around the Pacific Ring of Fire. Please people listen and prepare the Lord is returning soon.

In this book we established that God is real, Jesus Christ is the son of God, and the Holy Spirit is with us now. He gives us the knowledge and the power to choose life or death. The Angels of God are assigned to us and are protecting us. We learned that the spiritual realm is real. Demons roam the earthly realm and the spiritual realm. We saw photographic evidence of both, good and evil. God's Word is the truth, and He is real, so are demons, hell and heaven. Therefore, we have a need for a Savior, who saves our soul from sin and eternal spiritual damnation. We are made in God's image, body, soul and spirit. After we die, the body returns to the ground from where it was formed, the soul and spirit will go to God or hell, if we die in our sin. The soul is our intellect and the part that think's, feels. sees, tastes. Through God's Spirit this part of us is alive, if we are born of the water (by birth), and of the Spirit **(John 3:5).** This is called being born again, through the salvation and acceptance of Jesus Christ's sacrifice, as He died for our sins on the Cross. We being cleansed by His blood, we live after death. He became the sacrifice for our sins, so we can have eternal life. He became the Passover lamb, the blood sacrifice for our sins. So that our soulish body can have eternal life and return to the Father where it came from. **(Genesis 2:7)**

The proof that demons and angels are amongst us.

These are demons in spirit form, they have a spirit body. They see, walk, smell, taste. And as you can see, they have hairs, and a beard, and wear clothes. So are Angels in spirit form, they are clothed in the glory of God. We will be in spirit form when our body dies and we pass over into the spirit realm. The spirit realms, heaven and hell are real places.

Please stop with the wickedness, lying, unforgiveness, stealing, adultery, fornication, watching porn, and such, witchcraft of all sorts, worshipping idols. Please repent, turn away and turn to the only person who can save your soul, Jesus Christ.

Give your Life to Jesus Christ and be eternally Saved

Salvation Now. After we die, we will be in our spirit form and if we are not born again, if our spirit body has not received the forgiveness and salvation of Jesus Christ, we will join the demons in hell.

Salvation Prayer: Father, please forgive me my sins, wash me in the blood of your Son Jesus Christ, who died on the cross for my sins and died and rose again. Jesus be my Savior, I give you my life, come and be my Lord and lead me by your Spirit I pray, Amen.

.

John 3: 16 " For God loved the world that He gave His only begotten Son, that whoever believes in Him should not perish but have everlasting life."

Salvation is received by faith through grace.

Notes

Notes

Notes

www.ingramcontent.com/pod-product-compliance
Lightning Source LLC
Chambersburg PA
CBHW051235090426
42740CB00001B/26